JACK M____ E

TRULY
TER____
TALES

SCIENTISTS

h
Hodder
Children's
Books

a division of Hodder Headline

Text © Jack Marlowe 1997
Illustrations © Scoular Anderson 1997

First published in 1997 by Hodder Children's Books

The right of Jack Marlowe and Scoular Anderson to be identified as the author and illustrator of this work has been asserted by them in accordance with the Copyright, Designs and Patents Act 1988.

Designed by Don Martin

10 9 8 7 6 5 4 3

All rights reserved. No part of this publication may be reproduced, stored in a retrieval system, or transmitted, in any form or by any means, without the prior written permission of the publisher, nor be otherwise circulated in any form of binding or cover other than that in which it is published and without a similar condition being imposed on the subsequent purchaser.

A catalogue record for this book is available from the British Library

ISBN 0 340 66723 0

Hodder Children's Books
A division of Hodder Headline
338 Euston Road
London
NW1 3BH

Printed and bound in Great Britain by
The Guernsey Press Co. Ltd, Guernsey, Channel Islands

Contents

Introduction
page v

ARISTOTLE
A great Greek?
page 1

ROGER BACON
The mad medieval monk
page 23

JOHN DEE
The terrifying Tudor
page 43

FRANCIS GALTON
A truly terrible idea
page 65

iii

Also in this series

TRULY TERRIBLE TALES

Writers
Explorers
Inventors

More details at the back of the book

Introduction

'Science' is an old word meaning 'knowledge'... so those clever 'scientists' are 'people who know.' (And some science teachers are real know-it-alls!)

Except they don't know it all. They look at things and try to work out why they are the way they are. Why is the sky blue, and how

do cows eat grass and make milk? What happens if you put a match to gunpowder, and where do flies go in winter?

These scientists have been around for 4000 years or more. Ancient clay tablets show that people tried to work out how the stars move, what happens when you catch a disease, and what people are made of.

Those scientists had ideas. In 600 BC a clever Greek called Thales had a great idea and he said, "The Earth is a flat disc! It floats on water." The trouble is those ancient scientists didn't do experiments or tests. Old Thales didn't set off in a boat and sail off until he dropped off the edge of the Earth. (Would you?!?)

So, of course, the ancient scientists kept getting things wrong. Sometimes with truly terrible results, as these tales tell.

ARISTOTLE
384 – 322 BC

A GREAT GREEK?

1

Aristotle was a clever man and a good teacher. He is often called the "Father of Science" because he had so many good ideas. Some of his ideas were shown to be right two thousand years after he wrote them.

But, as with Thales, a lot of them were wrong ideas. Never mind, he passed them on to his young students. Bright young men like Prince Alexander, the son of the Macedonian king Philip. Put a wrong idea in the hands of a ruthless person like Alexander and some truly terrible things can follow.

The young Alexander was a clever boy, in his own way. But a science idea in his hands could become a deadly weapon...

THE PRINCE
and
THE POISON

The teacher took the bronze knife and struck the point down. It cut into the leathery skin of the dead pig and he sliced upwards. His pupils watched carefully. Prince Alexander's deep brown eyes glittered. "Did you kill the pig yourself, Aristotle?" he asked the teacher.

The man looked up sternly. "Certainly not, Alexander. I have no time for chasing around after animals. I am too busy with my work and my learning."

2

Alexander looked slyly at the other boy. "Just as well some of us like to hunt, eh Cleitus? Otherwise these teachers would starve."

Cleitus smirked. Aristotle's face was turning a little red under the thick, ash-grey beard. The boys enjoyed hunting but they enjoyed teasing their teacher almost as much. "Yes," Cleitus nodded. "I love killing pigs. Can we go out now and kill a fresh one for you, Aristotle?" he asked.

The teacher glared at him. "You will watch me cut up this one and you will see how the animal's body works," he snapped and was surprised to find he was waving the bloody point of the knife at the boy. He turned back to the pig and finished opening the skull. He stepped back. "This grey material here is the brain. Can you see it?"

"See it?" Alexander laughed. "I like to eat it!"

"What does the brain do?" Cleitus asked, as if he was interested.

Aristotle straightened and looked down his long nose at his two pupils. "The brain is a special organ for cooling the blood when it gets too hot," he explained.

Cleitus reached into the chest of the animal and pulled out the heart. "This is what I like to eat."

"That is the heart," the teacher began.

"I know," Alexander cut in. "But what does it do?"

Aristotle cleared his throat. "The heart is the home of the mind. The heart is where you have all your thoughts and all your feelings. When the heart stops then all feeling stops."

Alexander's faint grin faded. "And how can you make the heart stop?" he asked.

"You can damage it - stab it with a knife or spear - or you can put some substance into the stomach and it will stop the heart."

"You mean poison?" the prince asked quietly.

The teacher cleared his throat again. "Exactly. Poison. There are several plants which carry a deadly poison in their leaves and roots."

"Tell me some," Alexander said and his voice was cold as the rock the palace was built on.

The sun beat down on the tiled courtyard. It was hot in the shade where the lesson was being held but Aristotle shivered. There was something about the boy that made him uneasy. Some menace, some strange force. "No, Alexander. King Philip does not pay me to instruct you in poisons."

The boy shrugged his wide and powerful shoulders. "Cook will tell me."

Cleitus cut in, "So what does the king pay you to teach us?" he demanded.

"How to think," Aristotle replied promptly.

Cleitus sneered. "Anyone can think!"

The man's eyes glistened. This was the sort of argument he enjoyed. "Not true, young Cleitus! Not true! The power of thinking is not present in slaves!" he cried.

Alexander nodded slowly. "If they could think then they wouldn't be slaves," he said.

"Children cannot really think until they reach your age!" the man went on. "And women can hardly think at all!"

The prince blew out his cheeks, "My mother would not agree."

Aristotle shook his head impatiently. "Everything in the world has an order. At the top of the order are men!"

Alexander took the teacher by the elbow and led him out onto the terrace where Cleitus could not hear them. "But Aristotle," he said quietly. "Do men come in any sort of order?"

The teacher gazed over the sea that shone a deeper blue than any sapphire in the crown jewels of King Philip. "Yes, my boy! Men are at the top of the human order." He raised a hand to show a level. "But Greek men are higher." He placed his other hand above the first level. "Men from noble families are higher still."

Alexander placed his hand above both of Aristotle's, "And I am highest of them all?"

The teacher frowned. "Apart from your father, the king."

Alexander's eyes were hard as the tiles on the terrace. "Of course. My father. Can I never rise above my father?"

Aristotle smiled. This was what he enjoyed. Explaining his science to interested students. "Mix oil and water and what happens?" he asked.

"The oil floats to the top," the boy said.

"Exactly!" the teacher cried. "Everything rises to the top of its order. One day your father will die and you will rise to the top."

Alexander clasped the dagger that he carried at his belt. He stepped away from the low wall that overlooked the sparkling sea. "Where are you going?" Aristotle asked.

"To see the cook," the boy said.

"Your lesson isn't finished!" the teacher groaned.

Alexander gave his teacher a grim smile. "You have given me a lot to think about. Enough for today. Continue with Cleitus and the pig if you wish."

He turned on the heel of his sandal and strode into the palace.

"This pig is full of maggots!" Cleitus cried.

The last thing Alexander heard as he stepped into the cool gloom of the palace was Aristotle explaining, "They spring from dead flesh of any beast..."

It was a week before Aristotle saw Alexander again. The boy had changed in those few days. His open, friendly face was closed and hard now. The sharp eyes seemed to be hiding some clever secret. The teacher walked to the throne and knelt in front of his pupil.

"Your Majesty," he mumbled. "I was so terribly sorry to hear about the death of your father."

"Thank you, Aristotle," Alexander said smoothly.

"He died so quickly," the teacher said with a wondering shake of the head.

"Some illnesses are like that," the new king sighed and gave a signal for the teacher to rise and join him at the table. He poured a goblet of wine and handed it to the man.

Aristotle looked into the ruby liquid and his face was troubled. "You must excuse me asking... but... but some people are talking about... about..." and he whispered the word. "Poison."

Alexander's eyes turned slowly to meet the eyes of his old teacher. "I have heard that. I cannot imagine who would want to poison my father... can you?"

Suddenly Aristotle blinked. He was looking into the eyes of a stranger. Someone harsher than the boy he had taught just a week before. "No!" he said sharply. "No! No one! No one at all!"

The young king gave a slight smile. "Good. Good."

The teacher coughed gently. "So what are you planning to do now?"

Alexander had a piece of parchment on the table and pointed to it. "Do you know what that is?"

"A map. I may be a teacher of science but I know about all the other knowledge of the world," the man said proudly.

"It's a map of the world," Alexander said. "I have thought about what you said. Men rise to the top. Greek men rise higher and Greek nobles rise above other Greeks. But if Greeks are the best then a Greek should be able to rule the whole world!" The young man swept a hand over the parchment. "That's what I plan to do. I am going to test your idea, Aristotle. I am going to con-

quer the world. The whole world."

The teacher had a faint look of horror on his face like a man who has opened a door and let out some kind of monster. "One day they will call me Alexander the Great!" the young man said. "You can return to Athens, Aristotle ... your work is finished here. You will be well paid."

Alexander raised his golden goblet. "Your health, Aristotle!"

The teacher looked deep into the purple-red wine. He felt a tightness in his throat. "Thank you, your majesty... I'm... I'm just not very thirsty."

TRULY TERRIBLE SCIENCE
Aristotle was wrong, of course, when he said men were greater thinkers than women, and the noble Greek men were the greatest thinkers of all. It wasn't very good science. If he'd said something like "The moon is made of green cheese", it would still have been bad science, but it probably wouldn't have mattered too much. But when ruthless people like Alexander get hold of these ideas, they can turn a bad idea into something truly terrible!

No one is quite sure how King Philip died - but many historians think that his son had a hand in his death. Alexander the Great went on to conquer many countries - sometimes with terrible cruelty. Aristotle's ideas were sometimes horribly wrong. The idea that Greek men were meant to rule but that women and slaves could not even think is quite silly to us today. He was not a modern scientist - he never tested his ideas, remember.

That wasn't the only idea that Aristotle had. Here are ten more. Was he right... or was he wrong?

1

Drop
a heavy object and
drop a light object that
are the same shape.
The heavy object will
fall faster.

RIGHT OR WRONG?

2

Earthquakes
are caused by air
trying to escape
from the earth.

3

Meat
that is left will
grow maggots
from the
flesh.

RIGHT OR WRONG?

4

The Earth
is the centre of
the Universe, and
the Sun, Moon
stars go and
around it.

RIGHT OR WRONG?

14

5

The Earth
is not made up of
tiny particles
called atoms.

RIGHT OR WRONG?

6

Thoughts
come from the heart
and the brain cools
the blood.

RIGHT OR WRONG?

7

Men are
better thinkers
than women.

RIGHT OR WRONG?

8

The Greeks
are the greatest people
on Earth.

RIGHT OR WRONG?

9

The Earth isn't flat, it is a ball.

EARTH RIGHT SHAPE

EARTH WRONG SHAPE

RIGHT OR WRONG?

10

A scientist should collect all the facts possible.

RIGHT OR WRONG?

Answers

1 WRONG. People believed this for over a thousand years until a scientist called Galileo "tested" the idea by dropping objects off the famous tower of Pisa.

2 WRONG. Aristotle believed that everything tried to find its own level – Greek men rose to the top and slaves sank to the bottom. Air, Earth, Fire and Water were the same. Air always floated to the top. If any were trapped under the surface of the Earth, then it would force its way out as a volcano. Clever idea – but wrong.

3 WRONG. Maggots don't come from the meat. They come from eggs laid on the meat by flies. The eggs hatch to become maggots and the maggots grow to be flies. Of course, Aristotle did not have a microscope and the fly eggs were just too small for him to see.

4 WRONG. It was a better idea than the flat Earth belief but it was still wrong. Strangely, there were Greeks who believed that the Earth went around the Sun – which is right – but hardly anyone in ancient times believed them!

5 WRONG. The Greek Democritus said the Earth was made up of atoms. Clever Democritus was right even though he didn't have the tests to prove it. Aristotle scoffed at the idea. He said everything on earth was made up of Water, Air, Earth or Fire or some mixture of those things. The only other thing in the universe was something called Ether, which the stars in the sky floated in. Sorry, Aristotle... wrong again.

6 WRONG. Aristotle cut up more than 50 types of animals, insects, birds and fish to find out how they worked. But many of his guesses about bodies were wrong.

7 WRONG. A lot of men agreed with Aristotle when he said they had better brains that women - many men still believe it. As a result, women in the ancient world were not usually taught to read or write. Women (and sensible men) think Aristotle was very wrong indeed.

8 WRONG. The idea that one group of people is better than another group has caused a lot of misery for thousands of years. The people who think they are better try to prove it by attacking others. Alexander conquered the Persians, but the Romans conquered the Greeks, and so it went on. This was one of Aristotle's worst ideas!

9 RIGHT. He knew an eclipse of the moon was caused by the shadow of the Earth. That shadow was curved so the Earth must be curved.

10 RIGHT. And this is why Aristotle is the Father of Science. He made a lot of mistakes, but he showed the rest of the human race how to study the world around them. "Don't make up your mind till you have all the facts," is still useful today.

Aristotle returned to Athens to teach while Alexander went on to try and conquer the world. Not only did he massacre whole cities, but he also killed the friend who saved his life in battle - Cleitus. As he travelled he never forgot his old teacher. He sent animals to Greece for Aristotle's zoo!

Alexander defeated the mighty Persian Empire before he marched on to India. In the end, Alexander was conquered by his own greed - over-eating at a banquet made him ill and he died shortly after. Some people believe he may have been poisoned. He was only 32 years old.

The Greeks had hated the ruthless Alexander. After his death they looked for people to blame. People like Aristotle. The old teacher retired to the safety of Euboea Island, where he died at the age of 62, just a year after his famous pupil.

ROGER BACON
1214 - 1294

The mad
medieval monk

Roger Bacon was an English monk who joined the Franciscans. (They followed the teaching of St Francis of Assisi, the peaceful little man who talked to birds and animals.)

The Franciscans were keen on learning and education. That sounds boring, but it got them into a few exciting situations. It was Franciscan monks who went with Christopher Columbus when he discovered America. And it got Roger Bacon into prison for ten years! Being a scientist is a dangerous business. It's all very well to make scientific discoveries, but if powerful people disagree with you then they can lock you away to shut you up. The Franciscans banned his books because they said his ideas were against the Christian religion.

Just like Aristotle, Roger the monk had some wacky ideas. He believed you could read the future from the stars. Nothing odd about that - people today still believe the horoscopes they read in the news-papers - but it can't be tested or proved, so it isn't science.

Still, Roger read a lot of Arab science and brought a lot of Arab inventions to Europe. He also made new discoveries of his own and explained how the sun and the moon always look bigger when they are just rising. Can you explain it?

Roger Bacon said some pretty nasty things about the church leaders and that's what got him into trouble. But how did they find out? If one of his assistants had kept a diary, it might have told us...

SELLING BACON

14 APRIL 1378

I leaned over the balcony and looked down into the church where the older monks were praying. The candle in my hand sizzled and spat as I tipped it gently and watched the hot wax drip over. The first splash hit old Brother Armand on the sleeve of his habit and he didn't notice.

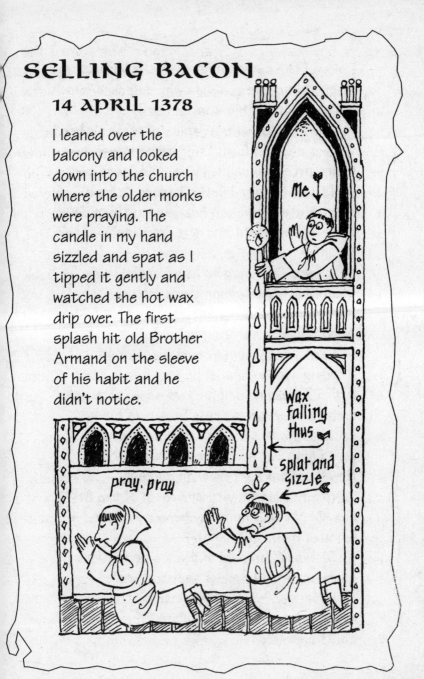

Me ↓

Wax falling thus ✍

splat and sizzle ←

pray, pray

I moved the candle a little to the left. It dripped and the scalding wax smacked him in the middle of his shaved head.

The old fool gave a little cry of pain while I turned and ran from the gallery. It was two hours after midnight, I was cold, I was bored and I was hungry. I never wanted to be a monk but my parents had died in the plague when I was a child and the Franciscans took me in.

So you can imagine how worried I was when Brother Stephen came into the dormitory, shook my shoulder and said, "The Abbott wants to see you."

Last time young Robert was caught dripping wax on heads, he was flogged and left in a freezing cell for two weeks with only bread and water to eat. That was funny because I was the one who'd dripped the wax. I just lied and blamed stupid Robert. Now it looked as if I'd been caught.

I went miserably to the room of the fat old Abbott and hung my head as I stood in front of him.

"Edward," he said in a voice as hard as steel on flint. "I have a task for you."

I guessed it would be cleaning the pig sties on my hands and knees. "Yes, father," I said miserably.

"You know Brother Roger Bacon ?" he said.

I looked up. "Yes, father. He works in the room with locked doors and secrets," I whispered.

The Abbott nodded and his chins rippled like waves on the lake in a storm. "Brother Roger needs an assistant to help with what he calls 'experiments.' I want to send you."

That cheered me up. "Because I am intelligent, hard-working and loyal?" I asked.

"No. Because you are a wicked, lying evil little weasel!" he roared.

I opened my mouth in surprise and it flapped like a pike in the pond. He just went on, "I know all about you, Edward. You splash hot wax on the heads of praying monk …"

"I don't!" I whimpered.

"And, even worse, you let pathetic little Robert take the blame," he went on. "I know these things and I have been watching you. I am sending you to work for Brother Roger Bacon because you will make a perfect spy. I want you to find out what he is up to and report back to me every day. You understand?"

Suddenly I understood. "Why should I?" I asked.

"Because you will be well rewarded with good food and a warm room. You will also be excused those prayer services that you hate so much." He smiled and I returned the smile.

"Can I start today?" I asked.

His little eyes sparkled in the folds of fat. "You can," he said. "And I want you to keep a diary."

This is it.

15 APRIL 1378

Brother Roger Bacon is mad. He wears pieces of glass in front of his eyes. He says his eyes are weak and the glasses help him to read and write. But when I look at him

they make his eyes big and scary. My first tasks are to clear away after his 'experiments'. I have to laugh. I thought I'd get the job of clearing up after pigs and sure enough, here I am clearing up after Bacon!

Brother Roger does not like jokes. As I put away his secret books he caught me looking at them. "They are in a code, Edward," he explained. "You could not understand them."

I just nodded and asked, "What do you do in here, brother?"

He looked at me through those discs of glass and said, "I am trying to find the secrets of how the world works."

"God makes it work!" I said. "He can do everything."

"Can he turn lead into gold?" the man asked me.

"He can if he wants," I said. "Jesus turned water into wine!"

"Exactly!" he cried. "So if God can do it, so can we!"

Ha! He thinks he's as clever as God! The Abbott would love to hear that! I remembered it.

Brother Roger made me sit next to him at his desk and took out a book. "It is an ancient art called Alchemy," he explained as he opened the book full of strange writing and drawings. "All we need to do is find a material called Elixir. When we add Elixir to lead, then we can make gold! One grain will turn a million grains of lead into gold. And when we have Elixir, then we have the secret of life itself. The man who discovers Elixir will live forever!"

"Like God?" I asked.

"Like God," Brother Roger agreed.

I told the Abbott about the experiments and he smiled a fat little smile and told me a story. "A thousand years ago a magician was boiling a strange mixture in a pot and trying to find this Elixir stuff. When he looked up he saw the devil at the window. The magician rushed out and grabbed the devil by the tail. The tail snapped off. The magician threw it in the pot and what do you think the mixture turned to?"

"Gold?" I guessed.

"Gold!" The abbot cried. "The Elixir and the alchemy are work of the Devil, Edward. You've done well! Help yourself to this chicken. Find out more tomorrow."

16 APRIL 1378

Today mad Brother Roger told me about his other dreams. He is so mad he frightens me.

31

"Edward," he said as we drank watered wine with cheese for breakfast. "Do you see that bird?"

A sparrow was fluttering round the monastery garden. I nodded.

"One day men will be able to fly!" he said.

"And pigs too, I suppose," I said. It was meant to be a joke, but he thought about it hard.

"Perhaps. I'm sure mankind can come up with a machine that will allow pigs to fly," he replied.

"What's a machine?" I asked.

"Something that works without human power. One day there will be carts that can run along the road with only a human to steer them. There'll be ships that will cross oceans at great speeds without sails or oars - even ships that sail under the water. Machines that can lift huge weights from the ground and move them somewhere else. Bridges over vast rivers that don't need pillars to hold them up."

Mad, quite mad, I thought. "Show me how to fly," I said quietly.

He took a sheet of copper and held it over a candle flame. "See the way fire always tries to climb upwards?" he said.

"Yes."

"Then we just have to fasten the fire beneath a metal umbrella and the whole thing will lift into the air!"

I shook my head. "No. If that were true we'd be

able to grab the straps of our sandals and pull ourselves above the clouds!"

He sighed. "You don't understand."

"I want to see it working," I said.

oink!

2 Mad Brother Roger's machines

His flying machine (mad!) ←

→ His horse-less cart (crazy!)

His boat without sails or oars (weird!) ←

His bridge that floats above the river (lunatic!) ←

"I am a scientist," he said. "I show how things work. It is for mechanics to make these things."

I left that night with a new report for the Abbott. "So," he smirked. "Pigs might fly, eh?"

17 APRIL 1378

Brother Robert met me on the way to Brother Roger's room this morning. "They say Roger had a statue of a head made of brass. It spoke to him!"

"It's not there now, you maggot," I told him.

"One night it shattered into pieces!" he squeaked then scurried off to his prayers like a two-legged rat.

I asked Brother Roger as soon as I went into his room. "Brother Roger, can you make things shatter?"

He squinted up through his eye glasses and said, "You have heard of my Chinese powder, then?"

I hadn't heard of it, but I said, "Can I see it work?"

He gave a yellow-toothed grin and said, "That is something I can show you. I make it from an ancient Arab recipe, and they learned it from the Chinese." He began to mix powders on a small metal dish as he talked. "One day we will be able to sail West and get to China, you know?" he muttered. "The world is a globe. Go far enough West and you reach the East!"

I gave a weak smile at his silliness. Finally he had a pile of grey powder on his dish. He passed me a wax taper that was glowing red on the end. "Touch the powder with the taper," he said. I reached forward as he was saying, "But don't get your face too close!"

He was too late with his warning. Lightning flashed in the dish and thunder clapped in my ears till they hurt. I could smell burning. As I ran to the door, the mad monk was crying, "One day the powder will be used on battlefields to scare the enemy!"

My sandals slapped down the corridor and didn't stop till I reached the Abbott.

"Where are your eyebrows, Brother Edward?" he asked with a smile.

"Bread and water," I cried. "Lock me away with bread and water! The man's a devil! He has made lightning from powder! He is a devil. Don't make me go near him again."

But the abbot smiled. "Thank you Edward. That is all we need to know to deal with the man. You have done well. You will be rewarded."

But I was sobbing on the floor. I never believed in devils till I met that man with his magic powder. Men won't fly and ships won't run on oarless engines. But believe me: one day Brother Roger Bacon's powder will kill someone!

Of course Bacon's powder became known as Gunpowder, and it killed countless millions over the centuries.

Bacon was imprisoned by his monastery for his science work, because the church saw it as black magic. Some of his ideas were as wild as Aristotle's - Elixir and gold from lead were just a dream. But the way he carried out experiments helped scientists to learn more and more about our world.

The magic makers

People in the Middle Ages were superstitious. If they couldn't explain something then they thought it was magic. If someone came along and tried to explain it, they thought he was a magician.

Roger Bacon was interested in the science of light. He was one of the first men in the world to wear glasses and used glass to bend light and make rainbows. The church said:

Bacon said:

A rainbow is made when water bends light. See! God doesn't come into it.

You can see why the Church wanted to lock him away!

But the biggest problem was that scientists all believed Aristotle's idea that everything was made of a mixture of Fire, Earth, Air and Water. Change the mixture and you changed the material - alter the mixture of lead and you could come up with gold! They really believed it.

On the other hand there were some crooked characters around who could sell the mystery of Elixir if they found someone daft enough (or greedy enough) to believe them.

Making gold the easy way

1. Take a small piece of gold.

2. Heat some lead in a metal dish over a flame until it melts.

3. Drop the piece of gold into the melted lead and leave it to cool.

4. Gather together some rich people - the richer the better.

5. Place the lead-gold mixture over a flame. Take some powder - chalk, flour or pepper, anything will do! Tell your audience, "This is Powder of Elixir" and sprinkle it on the hot lead.

6. Keep heating the lead till it boils away.

7. All that's left in the bottom of your dish is the gold that you dropped in the lead.

8. Show your audience the gold and say, "See! My Powder of Elixir has turned the lead into gold!"

9. Sell your Powder of Elixir for as much money as you can get. Charge them at least ten gold coins each.

10. Take your scrap of gold and take their gold coins. Go as far away as possible before they find out that they've been tricked. And the experiment has worked. You've made yourself a lot of gold!

Of course you are much too honest to ever do anything so wicked... aren't you? This sort of trickery has its dangers. Elizabeth I paid an alchemist to turn lead into gold the way he promised. He failed, so she had him locked in the Tower of London.

A similar trick was to put some gold dust in a hollow metal tube and seal the end with wax. Ordinary lead is melted in a dish and the metal tube is used to stir it. The wax melts, the gold dust falls into the lead and the audience think they've seen the lead turned into gold.

You may think the people who were tricked were ignorant because they lived in the Middle Ages.

But in 1783 James Price told many important people that he could make gold. He even believed it himself. When he failed he took poison and died from the shame.

Then a plumber made thousands of pounds from rich Germans because they believed he could make gold... and that was in 1929!

JOHN DEE
1527 - 1608

THE TERRIFYING TUDOR

Roger Bacon came from a rich family and spent a fortune on his science experiments. He probably joined a monastery because monasteries had the best libraries in the world at the time.

But science and religion, magic and money, were still being mixed together 200 years later in Tudor times. If an experiment worked then the scientists probably didn't understand why it worked.

Was it God? they asked

Or was it magic?

Some scientists had a third question... Is there any money in it?

The wizard's woes

John Dee was a clever man. He enjoyed experimenting and he enjoyed collecting books - he could have been a great scientist. But he also enjoyed amazing people, and that led him to being mixed up with some very weird people and some very weird business.

Towards the end of his life, John Dee had spent all of the money he made - or he'd been cheated out of it. No one would give him a job because they said he was a magician. Children were terrified of him because they said he was a wizard. In the end he was forced to write to his old friend Elizabeth I for help.

We don't have John Dee's letter to the queen. It may have gone something like this...

9 November 1592

Mortlake House

London

Your Majesty,

I hope my letter finds Your Glorious Highness in good health. There is no queen in the world so beautiful, wise and generous as Elizabeth I of England. It is no wonder people everywhere call her Gloriana!

Sadly your servant, John Dee, is not managing so well. I notice that Doctor Bennet is soon to become a bishop. I wondered if Your Gracious Majesty would consider granting me his old job in Winchester?

I have written down a report of my life so far - including many years spent in the service of Your Majesty. If your secretary would like to visit me he is welcome to read it and see how I, my second

Dee first became famous when Henry VIII was on the throne. He produced a Greek play and it was performed at Cambridge. In the play he created a miraculous effect in which one of the characters appeared to fly from the stage and soar up to heaven. This little trick earned Dee a reputation for being a magician and the name "magician" stuck to him for the rest of his life. It was the cause of most of his troubles.

He first met Queen Elizabeth when her sister, Mary, was on the throne. He told her fortune. Mary seized Dee and Elizabeth and locked them away – she didn't like fortune tellers, or half-sisters who might take her throne.

I don't like the sound of this horoscope! Lock him up!

John Dee spent miserable months in the Bishop of London's prison while Elizabeth was locked away at Hampton Court. He suffered the cold, bare cell and the night visits from the rats. But he was patient. He knew that Princess Elizabeth liked his work. He dreamed that one day she would be queen and he would be her fortune teller. But prison life could be truly terrible, and Elizabeth didn't always keep the promises she made. He may have tried to remind her of this when he wrote to her...

You may remember, I supported you against your sister Mary. As a result I suffered in a dreadful prison. My only comfort was to have Barthlet Green to share my cell.

Do you remember Barthlet? They said he was an enemy of the church and they burned him. I was there at the time. He died bravely, but horribly, along with all the rest that your blood-loving sister killed. They strapped bags of gunpowder to his legs so the fire would set them off and he would die quickly. Still, it was a horrible, horrible way to die.

I still remember the happy day when the cruel Mary died and you took her throne. And one of your first acts was to employ me. I used my knowledge of the stars to find the best day for your coronation. Now, predicting the future from the stars is a science and not magic. I am not a magician. At that point you promised to make me Master of St Katherine-by-the-Tower when Doctor Mallet died. Of course when Mallet died you gave the job to Doctor Wilson. I am

The truth is he went away bitterly disappointed, but kept trying to find ways to please his queen.

On his travels, Dee found a book on secret codes that proved very useful to Elizabeth's spy chief, Sir Francis Walsingham. The book allowed Walsingham's spies to read messages from Elizabeth's enemies. It was reading a coded letter that trapped Elizabeth's dangerous rival, Mary Queen of Scots and led to her execution. (They say she wore a wig at her execution and, when the headsman picked up her head, the wig

came away in his hand and the head crashed to the floor!)

Dee tried to please Elizabeth with new schemes and magical services. Elizabeth was grateful - but as careless about her rewards as ever...

By 1571 I had returned to my house on the River Thames at Mortlake and began to collect my library of science books and manuscripts. I did write to your Minister, Lord Burghley, pointing out that I had received no reward for 20 years of study. I even offered to use my sciences find a gold or silver mine in your kingdom. Perhaps Lord Burghley did not show you my letter.

Of course you did visit my house in 1575 to see my collection of books. Sadly my wife had died just four hours before your visit and you refused to step inside. But you did see my famous magic crystal that you had heard so much about. And in 1577 I was able to tell you the meaning of a comet that appeared in the sky.

It was the same year that my skills were needed to protect you from an evil plot - you may remember a wax figure of Your Majesty was found with a pin stuck

through the heart. I believe my
science saved your life.

I was promised a large reward,
of course. Your Majesty did say
that I'd receive £1000. For some
reason, less than half of that

Apart from mysterious powers, John Dee also
claimed to be a doctor and a dentist. Not all of his
dentist work was a success. He once offered to help

with the queen's toothache but she refused to have the rotten tooth pulled out. Bravely the Bishop of Lincoln offered to have his own tooth torn out to show how painless it could be! The bishop's jaw was broken by clumsy dentist Dee – and her majesty was not pleased.

In 1581 he began on his most important work. In that year he bought a crystal globe. Dee said it allowed him to see angels and speak with them. The people of London accused him of being a magician again and began to attack him in the street and in his home.

Soon afterwards he met a man called Edward. This man terrified the people of London with his close-fitting black cap that he pulled down over the back and sides of his head. (He wore it to cover his ears - or, rather, what was left of his ears. He had been accused of forgery and had his ears nailed to the pillory and cut off.)

Edward Kelly brought Dee even greater magic - and greater trouble...

Young Edward Kelly put me in touch with an angel. That angel found me a stone even more magical than my crystal! Of course, I had to pay Edward large sums of money to stay with me over the years.

A prince of Bohemia offered to pay us to work in his country and Edward and I went with him. That is when the great disaster struck. While we were away, the common mob of London invaded my empty house. They destroyed my furniture, my priceless books and my science experiments. They even took away a magnet that had cost me £33!

Dee and Kelly travelled through Europe again where they were often threatened with prison - or even execution! One prince said that Edward Kelly was a fraud and the spirits he talked to were just a trick of his voice. The prince was almost certainly right. They had to flee for their lives.

The men said that other princes offered them large sums of money to stay and work in Russia and Poland but they decided to return home to England. That's where Edward came up with a new money-making scheme. Dee tried to interest the queen in it...

On a visit to the county of Somerset, Edward discovered the magical substance "Elixir" at Glastonbury Abbey - the home of the famous King Arthur.

Edward cut a piece of metal from a warming pan and turned it into pure gold with the Elixir. The gold piece fitted perfectly into the hole left in the pan. Edward sent the pan, and the gold, to you. It proved that the Elixir turned metal into gold. I'm afraid you must not have received this wonderful example of our discovery for you did not reply.

In 1588 Edward left me to live in Bohemia and I have not seen him since. Sadly his magic stone and Elixir does not seem to work so well for me.

My friends have told me wicked lies about Edward Kelly. They said he was sent to me as a spy, to find out if I was dabbling in magic. They said he found that I was a weak and foolish man and he spent ten years robbing me of my money. They even tried to say that the angel's magic stone was just another fraud of Edward's and that

Dee had been tricked, but he didn't want to believe his friend Kelly was a criminal.

John Dee claimed to be a scientist, but Kelly made a fool of him, robbed him and left him penniless. All Dee could do was plead with the queen who had let him down so many times...

Edward has left and I am almost a ruined man. I have sold some of the jewels I owned, but still my wife and children are going hungry.

I know how kind and generous Your Majesty can be to her loyal servants. As I said, I would willingly take on the job of Master of St Cross in Winchester, or any other job you think may suit a humble but very loyal servant of such a mighty queen.

I look forward to receiving a reply to my humble plea.

Your loyal, honest and true servant

Elizabeth finally answered John Dee's plea when she received his letter. He was made head of a college in Manchester - where he argued violently with the teachers and the students.

John Dee's partner Edward Kelly was simply a crook. The amazing thing is that he managed to trick

John Dee for so long. It is even said that Dee didn't notice Kelly's missing ears for a long time! Kelly's magic stone seemed to work when Kelly was there... but Kelly left and John Dee couldn't get any messages from it. The angel voices were probably Kelly "throwing" his voice like an ventriloquist.

When the old queen Elizabeth died she was replaced by King James - a man who hated any hint of magic or witchcraft. King James even wrote a book about witchcraft and his own terrifying experiences. A so-called "magician" like John Dee was never going to be popular with King James. The old scientist died five years after the queen.

Dee himself seems to have been as honest as most Tudor scholars. He just suffered from the same problem as Aristotle and Roger Bacon... he never tested his ideas the way modern scientists do.

His experiments with magnets were science – his experiments with angels and magic crystals were superstitious nonsense. In Tudor times, many people couldn't tell the difference.

Tudor mystery

You can still see some of John Dee's science and magic equipment today. They are in the British Museum in London.

The report he wrote on his life has also survived so we know quite a lot about this strange man.

Try this quick quiz to learn a few more fascinating facts...

1 John Dee had a "magic" mirror that he used to call up his spirits. What was it made from?

A Gold.

B Coal.

C Glass.

2 John Dee was fed up with being called a wizard. He wrote to King James and said, "Put me on trial so the world can hear the truth. If I am guilty then...

A I will turn you into a frog."

B I will eat my holy stone."

C I will let you execute me."

3 When Dee went to Germany in 1578 he was given an unusual job by Elizabeth's ministers. What?

    A He had to secretly sell some of Elizabeth's crown jewels.

    B He had to spy on the German army and report back to Elizabeth.

    C He had to bring back a copy of a new book for the Queen.

4 John reminded people in England how important Maths was as well as Science. One of his tasks in Maths was to work out what?

A Exactly how many days, hours and minutes there are in a year.

B How far it is to the Moon.

C What the Queen is worth if her weight was gold.

Er...well, I suppose the stone is right.

5 Edward Kelly passed on orders from the 'angels' in his Magic Stone. (Of course the angels didn't exist and the orders came from Kelly.) In 1587 Kelly's Magic Stone ordered John Dee to do what?

A Share his house with Kelly.

B Share his money with Kelly.

C Share his wife with Kelly.

Answers

1 – B

The mirror was a black disc made from very highly
  polished coal. It was kept in a leather case so it
  would not become scratched. A black mirror
  must be strange to look into.

2 – C

Dee said he was an honest scientist and he would be
  glad to suffer the death sentence if anyone could
  prove he was in touch with the Devil. James
  ignored Dee's plea to prove his honesty, and the
  old scientist died a poor and hated man.

3 – B

Many people who travelled from England were
  asked to spy on the countries they visited. John
  Dee went to several countries and it was natural
  that he would be asked to spy. As usual he was
  promised rich gifts by Elizabeth... and, as usual,
  she forgot her promise to Dee and paid him
  nothing!

4 – A

Early sums about the length of the year were wrong.
  As a result, the Church experts reckoned the
  whole calendar was wrong by 10 days. John Dee
  did his sums and said it was wrong by 11 days.
  As a result of John Dee's sums, the change in

the calendar was held up while the Church experts argued. In the end they agreed with Dee. But it took them 170 years to decide!

5 – C

John Dee agreed to the Magic Stone's order to share his wife with Kelly. Lots of arguments followed and Kelly left England within a year. Dee never believed that he had been tricked and the two men wrote to one another until Dee died. Kelly then admitted that he had been sent to Dee to prove the scientist was a magician. He stayed because he could use the old man to make money. No wonder Dee died a poor man.

People like Dee and Kelly were feared by the ordinary people. Dee's home was smashed up as soon as he left it. Simple people thought they were destroying the work of the Devil.

Then King James came to the throne in 1603 and he also lived in terror of witchcraft. With the King and his people believing in magic, it was not long before anyone who experimented with powders and potions was being accused of witchcraft.

John Dee died just in time! Within a few years of his death there were terrible witch-hunts sweeping the country. Innocent people in England were hanged - in Scotland and Europe they were burned.

John Dee's jumble of science and superstition had

helped make people afraid. And frightened people can do truly terrible things like hang and burn others as "witches".

FRANCIS
GALTON

1822 – 1911

GOOD

BAD

GOOD BAD BAD

A TRULY TERRIBLE IDEA

Remember Aristotle, with his strange idea that men were better than women and that Greek men were best of all? Over 2000 years later, another scientist said men from Northern Europe were the best. His name was Francis Galton.

Where did he get this idea from?

From looking at himself!

He was a famous scientist and so was his cousin, Charles Darwin. "Aha!" Francis thought. "Two brilliant men in one family. It can't be luck. It must be something to do with us being English!" He created a new science called Eugenics, which tried to prove he was right.

The trouble is that some people took Francis Galton seriously. In 1924 the USA passed a law that said people from Eastern Europe and the Mediterranean couldn't come to their country - they weren't good enough. Imagine that! If Aristotle had come to New York and said, "I want to live in America," he would have been sent away. "Sorry, you're not clever enough."

Back in Europe at that time it was even worse. Adolf Hitler's Nazi Party decided their people were the best and it was fine for them to drive out people who were not so good. When it came to the Second World War in 1939 they went further and started to kill these innocent people. The main victims of the Nazis were Jewish people and about six million men, women and children died in their concentration camps. Sometimes the ideas of scientists can be truly terrible...

"NO ONE HERE."

Warsaw, Poland - 1943

"We are like mice," my mother said. "We hide here in the dark and try to live on any crumbs we find."

"Are the soldiers mice?" I asked. I was very young and very scared. The candle flickered on the bare table and made wide, sad shadows round my mother's eyes.

My sister Sophie answered, "No. The soldiers, they're the cats. They want to catch us. When

they do they'll eat us up!" She made a snapping sound with her teeth. I cried out loud and clung to mother's thin and faded dress.

"Hush now, Sophie," Mother scolded. "Joseph's young. He doesn't understand." Sophie shrugged. "He has to learn. A scared mouse is a mouse that runs and hides. But scared mice are the ones that stay alive."

"Would the soldiers really eat us, mamma?" I asked.

She brushed my hair with a cold, hard hand. "No, not eat us. But perhaps they'd send us all away."

"That's all right," I smiled. "At least we'd be together."

Sophie started to open her mouth to speak. Mother looked at her quickly. "They may not, Joseph," she said. "They may make you go to a different place."

"To a camp?" I asked. I'd heard about the camps. The children in our block talked of nothing else. "They'll catch you and they'll send you to the camp." We played some childish games of soldiers and children. The 'soldiers' chased the 'children' till they caught them then they put them on a train and sent them to a 'camp'. Then the game stopped. No one knew what happened next.

"What happens in the camp?" we asked.

The grown-ups never answered. All they said was, "Dreadful things. You wouldn't like it there."

"I don't like it here!" my friend Abraham complained one day while we were playing in the attics. "There isn't any food and the grown-ups never let us go outside."

"We go into the courtyard," I told him.

"That's not really outside," he said, and that was true.

The houses that we lived in were a hundred years or more old. They were five stories high and formed into a square. In the middle of the square was a cobbled space we called the court-yard. The grim grey buildings were so tall the sunlight never lit those cobblestones.

In the centre was a deep well. Grown-ups gathered round and talked. They never let us hear what they were saying.

The grown-ups sometimes went outside. They came back clutching little bags with hard black bread or sad potatoes. Other times they came back empty-handed. Then we went to bed hungry.

"Why don't we move to somewhere else?" I asked my mother.

"Ah," she nodded. "There's nowhere else to go. The soldiers would catch us and send us back. Or worse. They'd send us to the camp."

"We're safe here," Sophie said. She was just two years older than I was but she seemed so much wiser. She leaned forward and spoke quietly. "This block of houses is the only place where we are safe. There are a hundred ways to get in and out. Passageways the soldiers don't know anything about. Hidden doors that we can slip through."

"Yes, I know them all," I said.

"The soldiers come around from time to time. They look for men that they can take away to work for them. But when we see the soldiers come, we use the secret doors to hide away," my

70

sister said. "So many doors, the soldiers couldn't block them all."

"And so we play at cat and mouse," my mother sighed, "until this fearful war is over."

"When will that be, mamma?"

"When the British come. Or maybe the Americans," she said. That made me feel quite safe. I knew that somehow, sometime they would come and end our games of hide and seek.

"We're safe as long as we just stay in here," sister Sophie told me.

But Sophie was a child, like me. She did not know everything. Even Sophie could be wrong.

That late October day I'd sat out in the courtyard playing marbles on the cobbled ground. The sky was perfect blue above, but still I shivered in my thin grey jacket. Then the ground began to tremble and I wondered if my shivering caused it.

Someone hurried from a doorway, ran across the square and called out to an upstairs window. "Soldiers!"

The trembling was the tramp of steel-tipped boots on the road outside. I scooped my marbles up and hurried in to find my mother. Up the bare, worn wooden stairs along the landings filled with silent, hurrying people. "Soldiers, Mamma! Soldiers, Sophie,"

They were busy bundling up some scraps of food. They nodded. Mother grabbed me by the arm. We stepped out on the landing once again. A worried woman hissed a message in my mother's ear. She froze then slowly bent and whispered to us, "This time there are many, many soldiers. This time they will cover every way out. We'll have to hide and wait for them to go away."

"Hide where?" I asked and felt just like the mouse that's cornered by the cat.

"We'll go up to the attics," Mother said.

I knew that all the attics joined together. Those soldiers they could search up there for days and we could keep on moving, keeping out of reach of those cat-claws.

The whole of the building was climbing upwards. No one spoke. The only sound was the gentle

drumming of their feet.

Then the harsh crash of the soldiers' boots upon the courtyard. Orders shouted.

Mother stopped. "What's wrong?" I asked.

"Those voices. The voices giving orders. They were speaking Polish!"

"So what, Mamma?" Sophie asked.

"So... they're sending local people in to search the building. People who might know their way around!"

"But Polish people wouldn't help the soldiers," I said stupidly. "Why would anyone do that?"

My mother turned and hurried up the final flight of stairs. At last she stopped and waited by the ladder as people scrambled up towards the loft.

Four floors down I heard a door crash open. "Police!" a voice cried.

An old woman rested as she climbed the ladder. If she didn't hurry up I knew that we'd be caught. "Police," she said. "That's Sergeant Hasior."

"Yes, yes," my mother said. "I know. But..." Then she stopped. She couldn't bring herself to hurry up the poor old woman.

My mother turned to us. "Don't worry. They will start off on the bottom floor. Search it one room at a time. It will take quite a while before they reach this floor." She smiled and I felt safe.

At last it was our turn to climb the ladder. "We're the last," my mother said. "Should we pull the ladder up?" she asked.

An old man grunted in the dark. "No, don't do that. If they see that the ladder has been pulled up then they'll know we're here. Just leave it there."

And so we sat. We listened to the sounds of searching going on below. The crash of doors. Splintering wood when soldiers found a door that was locked.

The attic smelt of dust. I huddled next to Mother for some warmth. "When do we start moving?" I whispered.

"When we see which way they come. If they come from the left we move off to the right."

"And if they come from the right we move off to the left!" I said.

"That's right," my mother said and in the darkness I could feel her smile.

We waited while the sounds of boots on stairs and rifle butts on doors grew closer. Somewhere in the cold and suffocating dark a little child began to whimper. "Hush!" his mother said. "You'll spoil our game of hide and seek."

The child began to sniffle softly and I knew that he would give us all away. Mother's arm around my shoulders tightened as we heard the voices in the rooms below us.

"Search the attics!" came a voice.

We rose from sitting on the boards and crouched. The first crash came from on the left. I felt a gentle push and moved towards the right. The door was there. A little wooden hatch to let us in the attic on that side. I placed my hand against its rough surface and was just about to push when I heard the voice behind the hatch, "No one here, Hasior. Try the next one."

Soldiers were in the spaces on both sides. There was no place left for mice to run. When Sergeant Hasior climbed that ladder, we were caught.

Twenty people huddled in that little space up in the roof. You'd not believe that twenty people could make so little noise. Even the snivelling child was silent as the cat's paw on freshly fallen snow.

The ladder rattled. A heavy foot on the bottom rung made it creak. "Want any help, Hasior?" a voice called.

"No, sir," the policeman called back down.

I knew the voice now that I heard it. From time to time that man had walked around the courtyard, watched us at our games. He wore a dark blue uniform and thick black boots. I wondered how it would feel to wear such thick warm boots in winter when my own thin shoes let in the snow.

One day he'd trampled on a wooden doll that lay upon the cobbles. It splintered underneath the iron studs. It was Sophie's doll. Her only doll. He'd picked it up and thrown it in the drain.

Sophie cried that night.

I knew this cat was cruel. I knew that he would crush us as he crushed that doll.

His studs scraped against another rung and then another. Light spilled through the hatch and lit the dust-choked cobwebs. Still nobody moved.

Then a hand and arm appeared. It held a lantern up above the searcher's head. At last the head came into view

The grey-black hair. Thick black brows over deep-set eyes.

Twenty pairs of eyes stared at the head. Not one pair of eyes blinked or turned away. The Sergeant swung the lantern slowly round. His lips began to move. Perhaps the cat was counting all the mice he'd caught.

I caught his gaze. I looked into the face of death and thought those eyes were deeper than the courtyard well and twice as hard to understand. Five seconds we held that stare and then his eyes moved on. To Sophie, Mother and the rest.

Lantern shadows moved across the face and changed its stern expression. Suddenly a voice called up from down below. "Well, Sergeant? Anyone up there?"

A soldier's voice. A foreign voice. It spoke in Polish but with a foreign accent. Sergeant Hasior paused for just a tiny moment. A thin wafer of time that was all that stood between life and death. "No, sir. No one here. The attic's empty," he said.

Again the glance from those deep eyes swept round the room. And in the eyes an expression that could have been shame.

Then the head slipped down and the light was gone.

We sat in the dust-scented silence and heard the sounds of searching fade into the October afternoon.

That night we had a feast to celebrate. Not just bread but cheese to eat as well.

"Why did he do it?" Sophie asked again.

Mother shook her head. "Perhaps he's just a man," she answered.

In the corner of the room there was a soft rattle of tiny claws on bare boards. A bright-eyed mouse watched us as we ate. I broke a crumb of cheese off from the piece that I was eating. I threw it in the corner.

Anne died. Joseph lived and after the war moved with his family to England.

Galton's 'great' idea

Alexander the Great killed tens of thousands of people because he believed his science teacher, Aristotle.

Roger Bacon's experiments with gunpowder led to the deaths of millions when it was used as a weapon.

John Dee's magical experiments frightened people into hanging and burning hundreds of thousands of witches.

Francis Galton's ideas were not understood properly and led to misery and death for millions more.

None of these scientists meant any harm - they were all working to make life better for human beings! But sometimes science can be truly terrible.

Yet each scientist's experiments produced some good. Francis Galton, for example, was interested in criminals - he believed that criminals were "born" to be wicked. He measured and examined the bodies of people very closely and discovered one tiny but incredible detail... every single human has a different set of fingerprints!

This discovery gave police a huge weapon in the fight against crime. Francis Galton recorded over a hundred finger-prints of prisoners in 1893 but it was another nine years before the first criminal was caught using the system.

1. Denmark Hill, London, 1902.

Curses! The paint's wet!

2. Next day the owner made a dramatic discovery.

Someone's stolen my billiard balls!

And he's left a fingerprint on the wet paint on the sill.

3. Harry Jackson was reported trying to sell billiard balls in a pub...

Jackson, I arrest you for burgling a house in Denmark Hill.

I've never been to Denmark Hill. You can't prove a thing.

83

If you want to see how this works, then you can easily do some detective work yourself.

☞ Take a piece of black card or paper.

☞ Press a fingertip onto the paper

☛ Sprinkle talcum powder lightly over the spot.

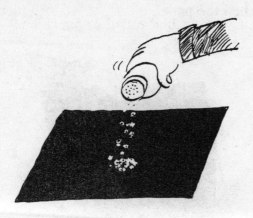

☛ Tap the card so the powder spreads.

☛ Tilt the card and keep tapping till the powder falls off.
The powder sticks to where your skin has touched the paper.

Why not challenge a friend? Ask them to secretly touch the paper with one fingertip. You should be able to tell which fingertip touched the paper.

Fingerprints are one of the millions of useful things scientists have taught us. With the help of scientists we have beaten dreadful diseases, brought happiness and comfort to billions. We have even put people on the Moon.

But every silver lining has a cloud. And sometimes... just sometimes... scientists can be responsible for truly terrible tales.

More Truly Terrible Tales for you to read!

TRULY TERRIBLE TALES

WRITERS

So you think being a writer is a nice, peaceful existence? Think again! This book delves into the action-packed lives and dramatic deaths of writers through the ages:

Roman horror king **Seneca,** whose own death is as nasty as his bloodthirsty plays ...

Bede, the Anglo-Saxon monk who tells of bloody battles and ghastly plagues ...

Tudor tearaway **Kit Marlowe,** star of his own murder mystery ...

and **Charles Dickens,** who shocks Victorian readers with his stories of cruel teachers and gruesome workhouses.

TRULY TERRIBLE TALES

INVENTORS

People invent things for all kinds of reasons: to save lives, kill their enemies – or get themselves out of trouble! This book tells the remarkable stories of real-life inventors with ideas of their own:

Ancient Greek **Archimedes**, creator of the deadly ship-smasher ...

Leonardo da Vinci, Renaissance genius – so brilliant, it's scary ...

Tudor inventor **Sir John Harington**, who flushes away a royal stink ...

and **Joseph Lister**, who sticks a knife into Queen Victoria!

TRULY TERRIBLE TALES

EXPLORERS

What makes someone risk everything to sail off into the unknown? This book tells the amazing stories of four real-life adventurers:

Brave **Pytheas**, the Ancient Greek. Can he sail to the end of the world without falling off?

Marco Polo, medieval sailor. He says he's been to China _ but is he lying?

Tudor toff, **Sir Walter Raleigh**, who discovers the potato, then loses his head ...

and fearless **Florence Baker**, Victorian explorer, who sees her own grave being dug!

ORDER FORM

0 340 66724 9 Truly Terrible Tales: Writers   £3.99 ☐
0 340 66722 2 Truly Terrible Tales: Inventors £3.99 ☐
0 340 66723 0 Truly Terrible Tales: Scientists £3.99 ☐
0 340 66721 4 Truly Terrible Tales: Explorers £3.99 ☐

All Hodder Children's Books are available at your local bookshop or newsagent, or can be ordered direct from the publisher. Just tick the titles you want and fill in the form below. Prices and availability are subject to change without notice.

Hodder Children's Books Cash Sales Dept
Bookpoint, 39 Milton Park, Abingdon, Oxon OX14 4TD, UK

If you have a credit card, you may order by telephone on (01235) 831700

Please enclose a cheque or postal order made payable to Bookpoint Ltd to the value of the cover price, plus the following for postage and packing:

UK and BFPO: £1.00 for the first book, 50p for the second book, and 30p for each additional book ordered up to a maximum charge of £3.00. Overseas and Eire: £2.00 for the first book, £1.00 for the second book, and 50p for each additional book.

Name ....

Address ....

....

If you would prefer to pay by credit card, please complete:
Please debit my Visa / Access / Diner's Card / American Express (delete as applicable) card number:

☐☐☐☐☐☐☐☐☐☐☐☐☐☐☐☐☐

Signature ....

Expiry date ....